Story-Tell Lib

Stories told by
Elizabeth Rowena Marietta York

Collected and recorded by
Annie Trumbull Slosson
in the early 1900's

Designed by
Nick Darien-Jones of
Nicholas J. Jones Graphics

Original monotype prints
and ink illustrations by
Bella Peralta

Published as a
collector's limited edition by
Darien-Jones Publishing

1st edition published 2011

Copy No. 7/500

ISBN 978 1 902487 05 2

Contents

*Dedicated to John Bowler, our design tutor, mentor and
inspiration from 1968 to 1972 – NDJ & BP*

Foreword

WHEN I moved into Hillside in 1994, the previous owner Eulalie Rodenhurst, gave me a book of parables told by Elizabeth Rowena Marietta York "Story-tell Lib" of Greenhills in the USA, which were collected by Annie Trumbull Slosson during the early 1900s. Eulalie wanted her book to stay at Hillside, hoping that I might use my skills as a designer to create a new edition of this little known treasure.

In 1901 Hillside was purchased by Eulalie's grandfather, a well-known local doctor, who sent many of the patients from his practice in Gloucester to convalesce at Hillside due to its healing qualities and uplifting views of the surrounding Cotswold hill country. So there seems to be a connection between Hillside – as a place of healing energy – and Lib's 'healing' stories.

Lib's stories are full of helping angels and have a universal quality, which has not been lost with time. Written down as told in a New Hampshire dialect, they have a resonance which innocently conveys the moral or spiritual meaning. They cry out to be illustrated and with this in mind, I asked a dear friend from art college days, Bella Peralta, if she would illustrate the stories.

Bella originates from the Cotswolds and has worked as a painter, illustrator and textile designer in California since 1974. She has exhibited her work widely in the USA and in Europe. Bella's multiple relief monotype prints and ink illustrations capture the real essence of Lib's "kind o' fables", by having surface detail and a wealth of underlying symbolism.

Nick Darien-Jones – August 2011

Story-Tell Lib

HAT was what everybody in the little mountain village called her. Her real name, as she often told me, ringing out each syllable proudly in her shrill sweet voice, was Elizabeth Rowena Marietta York. A stately name, indeed, for the little crippled, stunted, helpless creature, and I myself could never think of her by any name but the one the village people used, Story-tell Lib. I had heard of her for two or three summers in my visits to Greenhills. The village folk had talked to me of the little lame girl, who told such pretty stories out of her own head, "kind o' fables that learnt folks things, and helped 'em without bein' too preachy." But I had no definite idea of what the child was till I saw and heard her myself. She was about thirteen years of age, but very small and fragile. She was lame, and could walk only with the aid of a crutch. Indeed, she could but hobble painfully, a few steps at a time, with that assistance. Her little white face was not an attractive one, her features being sharp and pinched, and her eyes faded, dull, and almost expressionless. Only the full, prominent, rounding brow spoke of a mind out of the common. She was an orphan, and lived with her aunt, Miss Jane York, in an old-fashioned farmhouse on the upper road.

Miss Jane was a good woman. She kept the child neatly clothed and comfortably fed, but I do not think she lavished many caresses or loving words on little Lib, it was not her way, and the girl led a lonesome, quiet, unchildlike life. Aunt Jane tried to teach her to read and write, but, whether from the teacher's inability to impart knowledge, or from some strange lack in the child's odd brain, Lib never learned the lesson. She could not read a word, she did not even know her alphabet. I cannot explain to myself or to you the one gift which gave her her homely village name. She told stories. I listened to many of them, and I took down from her lips several of these. They are, as you will see if you read them, "kind o' fables," as the country folk said. They were all simple little tales in the dialect of the hill country in which she lived. But each held some lesson, suggested some truth, which, strangely enough, the child herself did not seem to see; at least, she never admitted that she saw or intended any hidden meaning.

I often questioned her as to this after we became friends. After listening to some tale in which I could discern just the lovely truth, which would best help some troubled soul in her audience, I have questioned her as to its meaning. I can see now, in memory, the shortsighted expressionless eyes of faded blue, which met mine as she said, "Don't mean anything, – it don't. It's jest a story. Stories don't have to mean things; they're stories, and I tells 'em." That was all she would say, and the mystery remained. What did it mean? Whence came that strange power of giving to the people who came to her something to help and cheer, both help and cheer hidden in a simple little story? Was it, as I like to think, God-given, a treasure sent from above? Or would you rather think it an inheritance from some ancestor, a writer, a teller of tales? Or perhaps you believe in the transmigration of souls, and think that the spirit of some Æsop of old, who spoke in parables, had entered the frail crippled body of our little Lib, and spoke through her pinched pale lips. I leave you your theories, I keep my own.

But one thing which I find I have omitted thus far may seem

to you to throw a little light on this matter. It does not help me much. Lib was a wonderful listener, as well as a narrator Miss Jane sometimes took an occasional boarder. Teachers, clergymen, learned professors, had from time to time tarried under her roof. And while these talked to one another, or to some visitor from neighboring hotels, little Lib would sit motionless and silent by the hour. One would scarcely call it listening; to listen seems too active a verb in this case. The girl's face wore no eager look of interest, the faded, short-sighted eyes did not light up with intelligence, nor the features quiver with varied emotions. If she received ideas from what fell upon her ears, it must have been by a sort of unconscious absorption. She took it in as the earth does the rain or the flower the sunshine. And so it was with any reading aloud from book or paper. She would sit, utterly quiet, while the reader's voice went on, and nothing could draw her away till it was ended. Question her later as to what was read or spoken of, and you gained no satisfaction. If she had any idea of what she had heard, she had not the power of putting it into words. "I like it. I like it lots," she would say; that was all.

Throughout the whole summer in which I knew the child, the summer which came so quickly, so sadly, to an end, little Lib sat, on bright, fair days, in a low wooden chair under the maples in front of the farmhouse. And it had grown to be the custom of her many friends, both young and old, to gather there, and listen to her stories, if she had any to tell. I often joined the group of listeners. On many, many days, as the season advanced, Lib had no words for us. She had always been a fragile, puny little creature, and this year she seemed to grow weaker, thinner, more waxen white, each day. She had a wonderful voice, shrill, far-reaching, but strangely sweet and clear, with a certain vibrating, reedy, bird-like quality, which even yet thrills me as I recall it.

I am going to tell you a few of the little stories, pictures, fables, parables, allegories, – I scarcely know what to call them, – which I heard Story-tell Lib relate. The words are her own, but I cannot give you the sweet tones, the quaint manner, the weird, strange personality, of the little narrator. Let me say here that often the little parables seemed meant to cheer and lift up Lib's own trembling soul, shut up in the frail, crippled body. Meant, I say; perhaps that is not the right word. For did she mean anything by these tales, at least consciously? Be that as it may, certain of these little stories seemed to touch her own case strangely.

The Shet-up Posy

HE first story I ever heard the child tell was one of those which seemed to hold comfort and cheer for herself or for humble little souls like her. It was a story of the closed gentian, the title of which she announced, as she always did, loudly, and with an amusing little air of self-satisfaction.

Once there was a posy. 'T wa'n't a common kind o' posy, that blows out wide open, so's everybody can see its outsides and its insides too. But 't was one of them posies like what grows down the road back o' your pa's sugar house, Danny, and don't come till way towards fall.. They're sort o' blue, but real dark, and they look's if they was buds 'stead o' posies, – only buds opens out, and these doesn't They're all shet up close and tight, and they never, never, never opens. Never mind how much sun they get, never mind how much rain or how much drouth, whether it's cold or hot, them posies stay shet up tight, kind o' buddy, and not finished and humly. But if you pick 'em open, real careful, with a pin, – I've done it, – you find they're dreadful pretty inside.

You couldn't see a posy that was finished off better, soft and nice, with pretty little stripes painted on 'em, and all the little things like threads in the middle, sech as the open posies has, standing up, with little knots on their tops, oh, so pretty, – you never did! Makes you think real hard, that does; leastways, makes me. What's they that way for? If they ain't never goin' to open

out, what's the use o' havin' the shet-up part so slicked up and nice, with nobody never seein' it? Folks has different names for 'em, dumb foxgloves, blind genshuns, and all that, but I allers call 'em the shet-up posies.

Well, 't was onc o' that kind o' posy I was goin' to tell you about. 'T was one o' the shet-uppest and the buddiest of all on 'em, all blacky-blue and straight up and down, and shet up fast and tight. — Nobody'd ever dream't was pretty inside. And the funniest thing, it didn't know 't was so itself! It thought 't was a mistake somehow, thought it had oughter been a posy, and was begun for one, but wa'n't finished, and 't was terr'ble unhappy. It knew there was pretty posies all 'round there, goldenrod and purple daisies and all; and their inside was the right side, and they was proud of it, and held it open, and showed the pretty lining, all soft and nice with the little fuzzy yeller threads standin' up, with little balls on their tip ends. And the shet-up posy felt real bad; not mean and hateful and begrudgin', you know, and wantin' to take away the nice part from the other posies, but sorry, and kind o' 'shamed.

"Oh, deary me!" she says, — I most forgot to say 't was a girl posy, — "deary me, what a humly, skimpy, awk'ard thing I be! I ain't more half made; there ain't no nice, pretty lining inside o' me, like them other posies; and on'y my wrong side shows, and that's jest plain and common. I can't chirk up folks like the goldenrod and daisies does. Nobody won't want to pick me and carry me home. I ain't no good to anybody, and I never shall be."

So she kep' on, thinkin' these dreadful sorry thinkin's, and most wishin' she'd never been made at all. You know 't wa'n't jest at fust she felt this way. Fust she thought she was a bud, like lots o' buds all 'round her, and she lotted on openin' like they

did. But when the days kep' passin' by, and all the other buds
opened out, and showed how pretty they was, and she didn't
open, why, then she got – terr'ble discouraged; and I don't
wonder a mite. She'd see the dew a-layin' soft and cool on the
other posies' faces, and the sun a-shinin' warm on 'em as they
held 'em up, and sometimes she'd see a butterfly come down
and light on 'em real soft, and kind o' put his head down to 'em,
's if he was kissin' 'em, and she thought 't would be powerful
nice to hold her face up to all them pleasant things. But she
couldn't.

But one day, afore she'd got very old, 'fore she'd dried up or
fell off, or anything like that, she see somebody comin' along
her way. 'T was a man, and he was lookin' at all the posies real
hard and partic'lar, but he wasn't pickin' any of 'em. Seems 's
if he was lookin' for somethin' diff'rent from what he see, and
the poor little shet-up posy begun to wonder what he was arter.
Bimeby she braced up, and she asked him about it in her shet-
up, whisp'rin' voice. And says he, the man says: "I'm a-pickin'
posies. That's what I work at most o' the time. 'T ain't for
myself;" he says, "but the one I work for. I'm on'y his help. I
run errands and do chores for him, and it's a partic'lar kind
o' posy he's sent me for to-day." "What for does he want 'em?"
says the shetup posy. "Why, to set out in his gardin," the man
says. "He's got the beautif'lest gardin you never see, and I pick
posies for 't." "Deary me," thinks she to herself; "I jest wish he'd
pick me. But I ain't the kind, I know." And then she says, so soft
he can't hardly hear her, "What sort o' posies is it you're arter
this time?" "Well," says the man, "it's a dreadful sing'lar order
I've got to-day. I got to find a posy that's handsomer inside than
't is outside, one that folks ain't took no notice of here, 'cause
't was kind o' humly and queer to look at, not knowin' that

inside 't was as handsome as any posy on the airth. Seen any o' that kind?" says the man.

Well, the shet-up posy was dreadful worked up. "Deary dear!" she says to herself, "now if they'd on'y finished me off inside! I'm the right kind outside, humly and queer enough, but there's nothin' worth lookin' at inside, – I'm certin sure o' that." But she didn't say this nor anything else out loud, and bimeby, when the man had waited, and didn't get any answer, he begun to look at the shet-up posy more partic'lar, to see why she was so mum. And all of a suddent he says, the man did, "Looks to me 's if you was some-thin' that kind yourself; ain't ye?" "Oh, no, no, no!" whispers the shetup posy. "I wish I was, I wish I was. I'm all right outside, humly and awk'ard, queer 's I can be, but I ain't pretty inside, – oh! I most know I ain't." "I ain't so sure o' that myself," says the man, "but I can tell in a jiffy." "Will you have to pick me to pieces?" says the shet-up posy. "No, ma'am," says the man; "I've got a way o' tellin', the one I work for showed me." The shet-up posy never knowed what he done to her. I don't know myself, but 't was somethin' soft and pleasant, that didn't hurt a mite, and then the man he says, "Well, well, well!" That's all he said, but he took her up real gentle, and begun to carry her away. "Where be ye takin' me?" says the shet-up posy. "Where ye belong," says the man; "to the gardin o' the one I work for," he says. "I didn't know I was nice enough inside," says the shet-up posy, very soft and still. "They most gen'ally don't," says the man.

The Horse that B'leeved he'd Get there

AMONG those who sometimes came to listen to little Lib's allegories was Mary Ann Sherman, a tall, dark, gloomy woman who was the daughter of old Deacon Sherman, a native of the village, who had died by his own hand, after suffering many years from a sort of religious melancholia. Whether the trouble was hereditary and his daughter was born with a tendency inherited from her father, or whether she was influenced by what she had heard of his life, and death, I do not know. But she was a dreary creature with never a smile or a hopeful look upon her dark face. Nothing to her was right or good; this world was a desert, her friends had all left her, strangers looked coldly upon her. As for the future, there was nothing to look forward to in this world or the next. As Dave Moony, the village cynic, said, "Mary Ann wa'n't proud or set up about nothin' but bein' the darter of a man that had c'mitted the onpar'nable sin." Poor woman! Her eyes were blinded to all the beauty and brightness of this world, to the hope and love and joy of the next. What wonder that one day, as she paused in passing the little group gathered around Lib, and the child began the little story I give below, I thought it well fitted to the gloomy woman's case!

You've seen them thrashin' machines they're usin' round here. The sort, you know, where the horses keep steppin' up a board thing 's if they was climbin' up-hill or goin' up a pair o' stairs, only they don't never get along a mite; they keep right in the

same place all the time, steppin' and steppin', but never gittin' on.

Well, I knew a horse once, that worked on one o' them things. His name was Jack, and he was a nice horse. First time they put him on to thrash, he didn't know what the machine was, and he walked along and up the boards quick and lively, and he didn't see why he didn't get on faster. There was a horse side of him named Billy, a kind o' frettin', cross feller, and he see through it right off.

"Don't you go along," he says to Jack; "'t ain't no use; you won't never get on, they're foolin' us, and I won't give in to 'em." So Billy he hung back and shook his head, and tried to get away, and to kick, and the man whipped him, and hollered at him. But Jack, he went on quiet and quick and pleasant, steppin' away, and he says softly to Billy, "Come along," he says; "it's all right, we'll be there bimeby. Don't you see how I'm gittin' on a'ready?" And that was the ways things went every day.

Jack never gin up; he climbed and climbed, and walked and walked, jest 's if he see the place he was goin' to, and 's if it got nearer and nearer. And every night, when they took him off, he was as pleased with his day's journey 's if he'd gone twenty mile. "I've done first-rate to-day," he says to cross, kickin' Billy. "The roads was good, and I never picked up a stone nor dropped a shoe, and I got on a long piece. I'll be there pretty soon," says he. "Why," says Billy, "what a foolish fellow you be! You've been in the same place all day, and ain't got on one mite. What do you mean by *there?* Where is it you think you're goin', anyway?"

"Well, I don't 'zackly know," says Jack, "but I'm gittin' there real spry. I 'most see it one time to-day." He didn't mind Billy's laughin' at him, and tryin' to keep him from bein' sat'sfied. He jest went on tryin' and tryin' to get there, and hopin' and believin' he would after a spell. He was always peart and comfortable, took his work real easy, relished his victuals and drink, and slept first rate nights. But Billy he fretted and scolded and kicked and bit, and that made him hot and tired, and got him whipped, and hollered at, and pulled, and yanked. You see, he hadn't got anything in his mind to chirk him up, for he didn't believe anything good was comin', as Jack did; he 'most knowed it wasn't, but Jack 'most knowed it was. And Jack took notice of things that Billy never see at all. He see the trees a-growin', and heered the birds a-singin', and Injun Brook a-gugglin' along over the stones, and he watched the butterflies a-flyin', and sometimes a big yeller 'n black one would light right on his back. Jack took notice of 'em all, and he'd say, "I'm gettin' along now, certin sure, for there's birds and posies and flyin' things here I never see back along. I guess I'm most there." "There, there!" Billy 'd say. "Where is it anyway? I ain't never seen any o' them posies and creaturs you talk about, and I'm right side of you on these old boards the whole time."

And all the children round there liked Jack. They'd watch the two horses workin', and they see Billy all cross and skittish, holdin' back and shakin' his head and tryin' to kick, never takin' no notice o' them nor anything. And, again, they see Jack steppin' along peart and spry, pleasant and willin', turnin' his head when they come up to him, and lookin' friendly at em out of his kind brown eyes, and they'd say, the boys and girls would, "Good Jack! nice old Jack!" and they'd pat him, and give him an apple, or a carrot, or suthin' good. But they didn't give Billy any. They didn't like his ways, and they was 'most afraid he'd bite their fingers. And Jack would say, come evenin', "It's gittin' nicer and nicer we get further on the road, – ain't it? Folks is pleasanter speakin', and the victuals 'pears better flavored, and things is comforfabler every way, seems 's if; and I jedge by that we're 'most there." But Billy 'd say, a-grumblin' away, "It's worse 'n worse, – young ones a-botherin' my life out o' me, and the birds a-jabberin' and the posies a-smellin' till my head aches. Oh, deary me! I'm 'most dead." So 't went on and kep' on. Jack had every mite as hard work as Billy, but he didn't mind it, he was so full o' what was comin' and how good 't would be to get there. And 'cause he was pleasant and willin' and worked so good, and 'cause he took notice o' all the nice things round him, and see new ones every day, he was treated real kind, and never got tired and used up and low in his mind like Billy. Even the flies didn't pester him 's they done Billy, for he on'y said, when he felt 'em bitin' and crawlin', "Dog-days is come," says he, "for here's the flies worse and worse. So the summer's most over, and I'll get there in a jiffy now."

"What am I stoppin' for, do you say, 'Miry? 'Cause that's all. You needn't make sech a fuss, child'en. It's done, this story is, I tell ye. Leastways I don't know any more on it. I told you all about them two horses, and which had a good time and which didn't, and what 't was made the differ'nce 'twixt 'em. But you want to know whether Jack got there. Well, I don't know no more 'n the horses did what *there* was, but in my own mind I b'leeve he got it. Mebbe 't was jest dyin' peaceful and quiet, and restin' after all that steppin' and climbin'. He'd-a-liked that, partic'lar when he knowed the folks was sorry to have him go, and would allus rec'lect him. Mebbe 't was jest livin' on and on, int'rested and enjoyin', and liked by folks, and then bein' took away from the hard work and put out to pastur' for the rest o' his days. Mebbe 't was – Oh! I d' know. Might 'a' been lots o' things, but I feel pretty certin sure he got it, and he was glad he hadn't gi'n up b'leevin' 't would come. For you 'member, all the time when Billy 'most knowed it wasn't, Jack 'most knowed 't was."

The Plant that Lost its Berry

I T was a sad day in Greenhills when we knew that Susan Holcomb's little Jerusha was dead. We all loved the child, and she was her mother's dearest treasure. Susan was a widow, and this was her only child. A pretty little creature she was, with yellow curls and dark-blue eyes, rosy and plump and sturdy. But a sudden, sharp attack of croup seized the child, and in a few hours she fell asleep. I need not tell you of the mother's grief. She could not be comforted because her child was not. One day a little neighbor, a boy with great faith – not wholly misplaced – in the helpfulness of Story-tell Lib's little parables, succeeded, with a child's art, in bringing the sad mother to the group of listeners. And it was that day that Lib told this new story.

Once there was a plant, and it had jest one little berry. And the berry was real pretty to look at. It was sort o' blue, with a kind o' whitey, foggy look all over the blue, and it wa'n't round like huckleberries and cramb'ries, but longish, and a little p'inted to each end And the stem it growed on, the little bit of a stem, you know, comin' out o' the plant's big stem, like a little neck to the berry, was pinky and real pretty. And this berry didn't have a lot o' teenty little seeds inside on it, like most berries, but it jest had one pretty white stone in it, with raised up streaks on it.

The plant set everything by her little berry. She thought there never was in all the airth sech a beautiful berry as hern, – so

pretty shaped and so whitey blue, with sech a soft skin and pinky neck, and more partic'lar with that nice, white, striped stone inside of it. She held it all day and all night tight and fast. When it rained real hard, and the wind blowed, she kind o' stretched out some of her leaves, and covered her little berry up, and she done the same when the sun was too hot. And the berry growed and growed, and was so fat and smooth and pretty! And the plant was jest wropped up in her little berry, lovin' it terr'ble hard, and bein' dreadful proud on it, too.

Well, one day, real suddent, when the plant wasn't thinkin' of any storm comin', a little wind riz up. 'T wa'n't a gale, 't wa'n't half as hard a blow as the berry 'd seen lots o' times and never got hurt nor nothin'. And the plant wa'n't lookin' out for any danger, when all of a suddent there come a little bit of a snap, and the slimsy little pink stem broke, and the little berry fell and rolled away, and, 'fore you could say "Jack Robinson," 't was clean gone out o' sight. I can't begin to tell ye how that plant took on. Seem's if she'd die, or go ravin' crazy. It's only folks that has lost jest what they set most by on airth that can understand about it, I s'pose. She wouldn't b'leeve it fust off; she 'most knowed she'd wake up and feel her little berry a-hold in' close to her, hangin' on her, snugglin' up to her under the shady leaves. The other plants 'round there tried to chirk her up and help her. One on 'em told her how it had lost all its little berries itself, a long spell back, and how it had some ways stood it and got over it. "But they wa'n't like mine," thinks the poor plant "There never, never was no berry like mine, with its pretty figger, its pinky, slim little neck, and its soft, smooth-feel in' skin." And another plant told her mebbe her berry was saved from growin' up a trouble to her, gettin' bad and hard, with mebbe a worm inside on it, to make her ashamed and sorry.

"Oh, no, no" thinks the mother plant. "My berry 'd never got bad and hard, and I'd 'a' kep' any worm from touchin' its little white heart." Not a single thing the plant-folks said to her done a mite o' good. Their talk only worried her and pestered her, when she jest wanted to be let alone, so 's she could think about her little berry all to herself.

Just where the berry used to hang, and where the little pinky stem broke off, there was a sore place, a sort o' scar, that ached and smarted all day and all night, and never, never healed up. And bimeby the poor plant got all wore out with the achin' and the mournin' and the missin' and she 'peared to feel her heart all a-dryin' up and stoppin', and her leaves turned yeller and wrinkled, and – she was dead. She couldn't live on, ye see, without her little berry.

They called it bein' dead, folks did, and it looked like it, for there she lay without a sign of life for a long, long, long spell. 'T was for days and weeks and months anyway. But it didn't seem so long to the mother plant. She shet up her eyes, feelin' powerful tired and lonesome, and the next thing she knowed she opened 'em again, and she was wide awoke. She hardly knowed herself, though, she was so fresh and juicy and 'live, so kind o' young every way. Fust off she didn't think o' anything but that, how good and well she felt, and how beautiful things was all 'round her. Then all of a suddent she rec'lected her little berry, and she says to herself, "Oh, dear, dear me! If only my own little berry was here to see me now, and know how I feel!" She thought she said it to herself, but mebbe she talked out loud, for, jest as she said it, somebody answered her. 'T was a Angel, and he says, "Why your little berry does see you, – look there." And she looked, and she see he was p'intin' to the beautif'lest little plant you never see, – straight and nice, with little bits o' soft green leaves, with the sun a-shinin' through 'em, and, – well, somehow, you never can get it through your head how mothers take in things, – she knowed cert'in sure that was her little berry.

The Angel begun to speak. He was goin' to explain how, if she hadn't never lost her berry, 't wouldn't never growed into this pretty plant, but, he see, all of a suddent, that he needn't take the trouble. She showed in her face she knowed all about it, – every blessed thing. I tell ye, even angels ain't much use explainin' when there's mothers, and it's got to do with their own child'en. Yes, the mother plant see it all, without tellin'. She was jest a mite 'shamed but she was terr'ble pleased.

The Stony Head

WHEN little Lib told the story I give below, Deacon Zenas Welcome was one of the listeners. The deacon was a son of old Elder Welcome who had been many years before the pastor of the little church in a neighboring village. Elder Welcome was one of the old-fashioned sort not so common in these days, a good man, but stern and somewhat harsh. He preached only the terrors of the law, dwelt much upon the doctrines, the decrees, election, predestination, and eternal punishment, and rarely lingered over such themes as the fatherhood of God, his love to mankind, and his wonderful gift to a lost world. The son followed in his father's footsteps. He was a hard, austere, melancholy man, undemonstrative and reticent, shutting out all brightness from his own life, and clouding many an existence going on around him. I have always thought that his unwonted presence among us that day had a purpose, and that he had come to spy out some taint of heterodoxy in Lib's tales, to reprove and condemn. He went away quietly, however, when the story was ended, and we heard nothing of reproof or condemnation.

Once there was somethin' way up on the side of a mountain that looked like a man's head. The rocks up there 'd got fixed so's they jest made a great big head and face, and everybody could see it as plain as could be. Folks called it the Stony Head, and they come to see it from miles away. There was a man lived round there jest where he could see the head from his winder.

He was a man that things had gone wrong with all along; he'd
had lots o' trouble, and he didn't take it very easy. He fretted
and complained, and blamed it on other folks, and more partic'lar
on – God. And one day – he'd jest come to live in them parts
– he looked out of his winder, and he see, standin' out plain
ag'in the sky, he see that Stony Head. It looked real ha'sh and
hard and stony and dark, and all of a suddent the man thought
it was – God.

"Yes," he says to hisself, "that's jest the way I 'most knowed
he looked, ha'sh and hard and stony and dark, and that's him."
The man was dreadful scaret of it, but some ways he couldn't
stop look-in' at it. And bimeby he shet hisself up there all alone,
and spent his whole time jest a-lookin' at that hard, stony face,
and thinkin' who 't was, and who'd brought all his trouble on
him. There was poor folks all 'round that deestrict, but he never
done no thin' to help 'em; let 'em be hungry or thirsty or ailin',
or shet up in jail, or anything, he never helped 'em or done a
thing for 'em, 'cause he was a-lookin' every single minute at that
head, and seein' how stony and hard it was, and bein' scaret of
it and the One he thought it looked like.

Folks that was in trouble come along and knocked at his door,
and he never opened it a mite, even to see who was there. Sheep
and lambs that had got lost come a-strayin' into his yard, but he
never took 'em in, nor showed 'em the way home. He wa'n't no
good to nobody, not even to hisself, for he was terr'ble unhappy
and scaret and angry. So 't went on, oh! I d' know how long,
years and years, I guess likely, and there the man was shet up all
alone, lookin' and lookin', and scaret at look-in at that ha'sh,
hard, stony face and head. But one day, as he was settin' there
by the winder lookin', he heerd a little sound. I d' know what
made him hear it jest then. There'd been sech sounds as that

time and time ag'in, and he never took no notice. 'T was like a child a-cryin', and that's common enough.

But this time it seemed diff'ent, and he couldn't help takin' notice. He tried not to hear it, but he had to. 'T was a little child a-cryin' as if it had lost its way and was scaret, and the man found he couldn't stand it somehow. Mebbe the reason was he'd had a little boy of his own once, and he lost him. Now I think on 't, that was one o' the things he blamed on God, and thought about when he looked at the Stone Head. Anyway, he couldn't stand this cryin' that time, and he started up, and, fust thing he knowed, he'd opened the door and gone out. He hadn't been out in the sunshine and the air for a long spell, and it made his head swimmy at fust But he heerd the little cryin' ag'in, and he run along on to find the child. But he couldn't find it; every time he'd think he was close to it, he'd hear the cryin' a little further off. And he'd go on and on, a-stumblin' over stones and fall in' over logs and a-steppin' into holes, but stickin' to it, and forgettin' everything only that little cryin' voice ahead of him. Seems 's if he jest must find that little lost boy or girl, 's if he'd be more 'n willin' to give up his own poor lonesome old life to save that child. And, jest 's he come to thinkin' that, he see somethin' ahead of him movin' and in a minute he knowed he'd found the lost child.

'Fore he thought what he was a-doin', he got down on his knees jest 's he used to do 'fore he got angry at God, and was goin' to thank him for helpin' him to save that child. Then he rec'lected. It come back to him who God was, and how he'd seed his head, with the ha'sh stony face up on the mountain, and that made him look up to see it ag'in. And oh! what do you think he see? There was the same head up there, – he couldn't make a mistake about that, – but the face, oh! the face was so diff'ent. It wasn't ha'sh nor hard nor dark any more. There was such a lovin', beautiful, kind sort o' look on it now. Some ways it made the man think a mite of the way his father, that had died ever so long ago, used to look at him when he was a boy, and had been bad, and then was sorry and 'shamed. Oh, 't was the beautif'lest face you never see! "Oh! what ever does it mean?" says the man out loud. "What's changed that face so? Oh! what in the world's made it so diff'ent?" And jest that minute a Angel come up close to him. 'T was a little young Angel, and I guess mebbe 't was what he'd took for a lost child, and that he'd been follerin' so fur. And the Angel says, "The face ain't changed a mite. 'T was jest like that all the time, only you're lookin' at it from a diff'ent p'int." And 't was so, and he see it right off. He'd been follerin' that cryin' so fur and so long that he'd got into a diff'ent section o' country, and he'd got a diff'ent view, oh! a terr'ble diff'ent view, and he never went back.

Diff'ent Kind o' Bundles

EVERYBODY in Greenhills knew "Stoopin' Jacob," the little hump backed boy who lived at the north end of the village. From babyhood he had suffered from a grievous deformity which rounded his little shoulders and bowed the frail form. It was characteristic of the kindly folk of the neighbor-hood, that, instead of calling the boy Hump-backed or Crooked-backed Jacob, they gave him the name of Stoopin' Jacob, as if the bowed and bent posture was voluntary, and not enforced.

A lovely soul dwelt in that crooked, pain-racked body, and looked out of the gentle brown eyes shining in the pale, thin little face. Every one loved the boy, most of all the dogs, cats, horses, cows of the little farms, the birds and animals of forest and brook-side. He knew them all, and they knew, loved, and trusted him. The tinier creatures, such as butterflies, bees, ants, beetles, even caterpillars, downy or smooth, were his friends, or seemed so. He knew them, watched them, studied their habits, and was the little naturalist of Greenhills village, consulted by all, even by older and wiser people.

A close friendship existed between the boy and Lib, and we all understood the tale she told us one day when Stoopin' Jacob was one of the listeners.

Once there was a lot o' folks, and every single one on 'em had bundles on their backs. But they was all diff'ent, oh! jest as diff'ent as – as anything, the bundles was. And these folks all

b'longed to one person, that they called the Head Man. They was his folks, and nobody else's, and he had the whole say, and could do anything he wanted to. But he was real nice, and always done jest the best thing, – yes, sir, the bestest thing, whatever folks might say against it.

Well, I was tellin' ye about how these folks had diff'ent kind o' bundles on their backs. 'T was this way. One on 'em was a man that had a real hefty bundle on his back, that he'd put on there hisself, – not all to onct, but a mite to time, for years 'n' years. 'T was a real cur'us bundle, made up out o' little things in the road that 'd got in his way, or hurt him, or put him back. Some on 'em was jest little stones that had hurt his feet, and some was little stingin' weeds that smarted him as he went by 'em, and some was jest mites o' dirt somebody 'd throwed at him, not meanin' no great o' harm. He'd picked 'em all up, every bit o' worryin', prickin', hurtin' little thing, and he'd piled 'em up on his back till he had a big bundle that he allers carried about and never forgot for a minute.

He was f'rever lookin' out for sech troublin' things, too, and he'd see 'em way ahead on him in his road, and sometimes he'd think he see 'em when there wa'n't any there 't all. And, 'stead o' lettin' 'em lay where they was, and goin' right ahead and forgettin' 'em, he'd pick every single one on 'em up and pile 'em on that bundle, and carry 'em wherever he went.

And he was allers talkin' about 'em to folks, p'intin' out that little stone that he'd stubbed his toe on, and this pesky weed that stung him, and t' other little mite o' mud he'd conceited somebody 'd throwed at him. He fretted and scolded and complained 'bout 'em, and made out that nobody never had so many tryin' things gettin' in his way as he had. He never took into 'count, ye see, that he'd picked 'em up hisself and piled 'em on his own back. If he'd jest let 'em lay, and gone along, he'd 'a' forgot 'em all, I guess, after a spell.

Then there was another man with a bundle, a cur'us one too, for 't was all made out o' money, dreadful heavy and cold and hard to carry. Every speck o' money he could scrape together he'd put in that bundle, till he couldn't scursely heft it, 't was that big and weighed so much. He had plenty o' chances to make it lighter, for there was folks all along the road that needed it bad, – little child'en that hadn't no clo'es nor no victuals, and sick folks and old folks, every one on 'em needin' money dreadful bad. But the man never gin 'em a mite. He kep' it all on his back, a-hurtin' and weighin' him down.

Then ag'in there was another man. He had a bundle that he didn't put on his back hisself, nor the Head Man didn't nuther. Folks did it to him. He hadn't done nothin' to deserve it, 't was jest put on him by other people, and so 't was powerful hard to bear. But, ye see, the Head Man had pervided partic'lar for them kind, and he'd said in public, so 't everybody knowed about it, that he'd help folks like that, – said he'd help 'em carry sech bundles his-self, or mebbe take 'em off, if it 'peared to be best.

But this man disremembered that, – or worse still, p'r'aps he didn't 'zackly believe it. So he went along all scrunched down with that hefty bundle other folks had piled up on him, not scoldin' nor complainin' nor gittin' mad about it, but jest thinkin' it had got to be, and nobody could help him. But ye see it hadn't got to be, and somebody could 'a' helped him.

And then bimeby along come a man that had sech a hefty, hefty bundle! 'T was right 'tween his shoulders, and it sort o' scrooched him down, and it hurt him in his back and in his feelin's. The Head Man had put that bundle on the man hisself when he was a little bit of a feller. He'd made it out o' flesh and skin and things. It was jest ezackly like the man's body, so 't when it ached he ached hisself. And he'd had to carry that thing about all his born days.

I don't know why the Head Man done it, I'm sure, but I know how good and pleasant he was, and how he liked his folks and meant well to 'em, and how he knowed jest what oughter be and what hadn't oughter be, so 't stands to reason he'd done this thing a-purpose, and not careless like, and he hadn't made no mistake.

I've guessed a lot o' reasons why he done it. Mebbe he see the man wouldn't 'a' done so well without the bundle, – might 'a' run off, 'way, 'way off from the Head Man and the work he had to do. Or, ag'in, p'r'aps he wanted to make a 'zample of the man, and show folks how patient and nice a body could be, even though he had a big, hefty bundle to carry all his born days, one made out o' flesh and skin and things, and that hurt dreadful.

But my other guess is the one I b'leeve in most, – that the Head Man done it to scrooch him down, so 's he'd take notice o' little teenty things, down below, that most folks never see, things that needed him to watch 'em, and do for 'em, and tell about 'em. That's my fav'rite guess. 'T any rate, the Head Man done right, – I'm cert'in sure o' that.

And it *had* made the man nicer, and pleasanter spoken, and kinder to folks, and partic'lar to creaturs. It had made him sort o' bend down, 't was so hefty, and so he'd got to takin' notice o' teenty little things nobody else scursely'd see, – mites o' posies, and cunnin' little bugs, and creepin', crawlin' things. He took a heap o' comfort in 'em. And he told other folks 'bout them little things and their little ways, and what they was made for, and things they could learn us; and 't was real int'restin', and done folks good too.

And, deary me, he was that patient and good and un-complainin', you never see! No, I ain't a-cryin'. This was a stranger, this man, you know, and I make a p'int o' never cryin' about strangers.

There was a lot and a lot more kinds o' folks with bundles, but I'm only goin' to tell ye about them four, this time, any way.

Well, come pay day, these folks all come up afore the Head Man to be settled with. And fust he called up the man that had the bundle all made out o' things that had pricked him, and tripped him up, and scratched him, and put him back on the road. And then he had up the man with the money weighin' him down, – the money he'd kep' away from poor folks and piled up on his own back. And then come the feller that was carryin' the heavy bundle folks had put on him when 't wa'n't no fault o' his'n, and that he might 'a' got red of a long spell back, if he'd only rec'lected what the Head Man had said 'bout sech cases, and how they could be helped.

I ain't a-goin' to tell ye what he said to them folks, 'cause 't ain't my business, seems to me. Whether he punished either on 'em, or scolded 'em, or sent em off to try ag'in, or what all, never mind. Knowin' 's much as I do about the ways o' that Head Man, I bet he made 'em feel terrible ashamed, any way.

But when he came to the man with the bundle made out o' flesh and skin and things, he looks at him a minute, and then says he, the Head Man does, "Why," he says, "that's my own work! I made that bundle, and I fixed it on your back all myself. I hefted and I sized it, and I hefted you and sized you. A mite of a young one you was then. I made it jest hefty enough for you to carry, not a bit heftier, no more nor less. I rec'lect it well," he says. "I ain't forgot it. I never forgot it one minute sence I fitted in on, though mebbe you kind o' thought by spells that I had.

And now," he says – No, I can't tell ye what he says. It's a secret, that is. But I don't mind lettin' ye know that the man was sat'sfied, perfec'ly sat'sfied. Ah Angel told me he was, and went on to say the man was dreadful pleased to find he'd been wearin' a bundle the Head Man hisself had made and fixed on him, heftin' it and sizin' it, and heftin' him and sizin' him too, so's 't wa'n't too much for him to carry. But he ain't carryin' it no more. The Angel said so.

The Boy that was Scaret o' Dyin'

I HAVE told you that little Lib was a delicate child, and that she grew more and more fragile and weak as the summer went on. In the hot, dry days of August she drooped like a thirsty flower, and her strength failed very fast. Her voice, though still sweet and clear, lost its shrillness, and one had to draw very close to the little speaker that he might not lose a word of the stories she told. Aunt Jane York often came out to us now, anxious and fussy, talking fretfully of and to little Lib, feeling the small hands and feet to see if they were cold, and drawing the shawl closer around the wasted form. I know she loved the little girl, and perhaps she wished now that she had shown that love more tenderly. She talked freely, in the very presence of the child, of her rapid decline and the probability that she would not "last long." Lib said nothing concerning her own condition, and showed no sign of having heard her aunt's comments. But one day, when Miss York, after speaking very freely and plainly of the child's approaching end, had gone indoors, Story-tell Lib announced, in a low, sweet voice, a new story.

Once there was a boy that was dreadful scaret o' dyin'. Some folks is that way, you know; they ain't never done it to know how it feels, and they're scaret. And this boy was that way. He wa'n't very rugged, his health was sort o' slim, and mebbe that made him think about sech things more. 'T any rate, he was terr'ble scaret o' dyin'. 'T was a long time ago this was, – the

times when posies and creaturs could talk so's folks could know what they was sayin'.

And one day, as this boy, his name was Reuben, – I forget his other name, – as Reuben was settin' under a tree, an ellum tree, cryin', he heerd a little, little bit of a voice, – not squeaky, you know, but small and thin and soft like, – and he see 't was a posy talkin'. 'T was one o' them posies they call Benjamins, with three-cornered whitey blowths with a mite o' pink on 'em, and it talked in a kind o' pinky-white voice, and it says, "What you cryin' for, Reuben?" And he says, "'Cause I'm scaret o' dyin'," says he; "I'm dreadful scaret o' dyin'." Well, what do you think? That posy jest laughed, – the most cur'us little pinky-white laugh 't was, – and it says, the Benjamin says: "Dyin'! Scaret o' dyin'? Why, I die myself every single year o' my life." "Die yourself!" says Reuben. "You're foolin'; you're alive this minute." "'Course I be," says the Benjamin; "but that's neither here nor there, – I've died every year sence I can remember." "Don't it hurt?" says the boy. "No, it don't," says the posy; "it's real nice. You see, you get kind o' tired a-holdin' up your head straight and lookin' peart and wide awake, and tired o' the sun shinin' so hot, and the winds blowin' you to pieces, and the bees a-takin' your honey. So it's nice to feel sleepy and kind o' hang your head down, and get sleepier and sleepier, and then find you're droppin' off. Then you wake up jest 't the nicest time o' year, and come up and look 'round, and – why, I like to die, I do." But someways that didn't help Reuben much as you d think. "I ain't a posy," he think to himself, "and mebbe I wouldn't come up."

Well, another time he was settin on a stone in the lower pastur', cryin' again, and he heerd another cur'us little voice. 'T wa'n't like the posy's voice, but 't was a little, wooly, soft, fuzzy voice, and he see 't was a caterpillar a-talkin' to him.

And the caterpillar says, in his fuzzy little voice, he says, "What you cryin' for, Reuben?" And the boy, he says, "I'm powerful scaret o' dyin', that's why," he says. And that fuzzy caterpillar he laughed. "Dyin'!" he says. "I'm lottin' on dyin' myself. All my fam'ly," he says, "die every once in a while, and when they wake up they're jest splendid, – got wings, and fly about, and live on honey and things. Why, I wouldn't miss it for anything!" he says. "I'm lottin' on it." But somehow that didn't chirk up Reuben much. "I ain't a caterpillar," he says, "and mebbe I wouldn't wake up at all."

Well, there was lots o' other things talked to that boy, and tried to help him, – trees and posies and grass and crawlin' things, that was allers a-dyin' and livin', and livin' and dyin'. Reuben thought it didn't help him any, but I guess it did a little mite, for he couldn't help thinkin' o' what they every one on 'em said. But he was scaret all the same.

And one summer he begun to fail up faster and faster, and he got so tired he couldn't hardly hold his head up, but he was scaret all the same. And one day he was layin' on the bed, and lookin' out o' the east winder, and the sun kep' a-shinin' in his eyes till he shet 'em up, and he fell asleep. He had a real good nap, and when he woke up he went out to take a walk.

And he begun to think o' what the posies and trees and creaturs had said about dyin', and how they laughed at his bein' scaret at it, and he says to himself, "Why, someways I don't feel so scaret to-day, but I s'pose I be." And jest then what do you think he done? Why, he met a Angel. He'd never seed one afore, but he knowed it right off. And the Angel says, "Ain't you happy, little boy?" And Reuben says, "Well, I would be, only I'm so dreadful scaret o' dyin'. It must be terr'ble cur'us," he says, "to be dead." And the Angel says, "Why, you be dead." And he was.

The story of the boy that was scaret o' dyin' was the last story that little Lib ever told us. We saw her sometimes after that, but she was not strong enough to talk much. She sat no longer now in the low chair under the maples, but lay on a chintz-covered couch in the sitting-room, by the west windows. The once shrilly-sweet voice with its clear bird tones was but a whisper now, as she told us over and again, while she lay there, that she would tell us a new story "tomorrow." It was always "tomorrow" till the end came. And the story was to be, so the whisper went on, "the beautif'lest story, – oh, you never did!" And its name was to be, – what a faint and feeble reproduction of the old triumphant announcement of a new title! – "The Posy Gardin' that the King Kep'?"

She never told us that story. Before the autumn leaves had fallen, while the maples in front of the farmhouse were still red and glorious in their dying beauty, we laid our little friend to rest. Perhaps she will tell us the tale some day. I am sure there will be "a Angel" in it, – sure, too, that the story will have a new and tender meaning if we hear it there, that story of the King and of the posy gardin' he kep'.

The illustrations in this book are available as 483 x 329mm (19" x 13") fine art reproductions from the publishers.

Darien-Jones Publishing
COLLECTOR'S LIMITED EDITION

Hillside House · Pitchcombe · Stroud · Gloucestershire GL6 6LN · England
Tel: (01452) 812550 · Email: djp@nicholasjjonesgraphics.co.uk